PRESENTED TO:

_____

FROM:

_____

DATE:

_____

FINDING MY HAPPY PLACE

Copyright ©2019 Joelle Brake

ISBN: 9781709488665
Independently published

No content in this journal, should ever be used as a substitute for direct medical advice from your doctor or other qualified clinician.

FINDING MY HAPPY PLACE

Finding My Happy Place

JOURNAL

AN ATTITUDE
OF GRATITUDE
LEADS TO HAPPINESS

FINDING MY HAPPY PLACE

The only person you should try to be better than is the person you were yesterday.
– Anonymous

● ● ● ●

Finding My Happy Place transforms the art of journaling because it focuses on three core components of your happiness journey:

- Awareness of your feelings and emotions
- Being conscious of what you already have
- Positive psychology

With quotes that inspire the heart, jotting down your thoughts in a simplistic format can lead to dramatic changes in your life. It shifts your mindset to an *attitude of gratitude*. This shift can lead to improving your overall happiness and well-being. Journaling is a commitment, that's well worth it! Set a routine. It can be daily, weekly, or whatever works for you.

The disillusion of sweating the small stuff led to the inauguration of my attitude of gratitude.

Best of luck on your journey,

Joelle Brake

FINDING MY HAPPY PLACE

Things to consider while journaling...

Feeling Words - Reflect on your entire day (the good, the bad, and even... the ugly). Think of one word that helps you describe your overall feeling for the day. There's a list in the tips section at the back of the book. You can use one of these or come up with your own.

Gratitude - You may be grateful for family or a job offer, but you CAN ALSO BE grateful that the barista didn't screw up your latte again. Gratitude comes in varying depths. Explore them! Get creative.

Positive Characteristics - You are awesome! Yes, you are. Don't wait for others to tell you. While the external affirmations may feel good at times, you don't always need them. There's a list in the tips section at the back of the book. You can use these or come up with your own.

attitude
[at-i-tood, -tyood]   noun
manner, disposition, feeling, etc., with regard to a person or thing; especially of the mind

gratitude
[grat-i-tood, -tyood]   noun
warmly or deeply appreciative of kindness or benefits received; the quality or feeling of being thankful

happiness
[hap-ee-nis]   noun
good fortune; pleasure; contentment; joy

An attitude of gratitude leads to happiness.

FINDING MY HAPPY PLACE

Living in the moment means letting go of the past and not waiting for the future. It means living your life consciously, aware that each moment you breathe is a gift.
– Oprah Winfrey

DATE _____   FEELING WORD _____

TODAY, I AM GRATEFUL FOR:

1. _____
2. _____
3. _____

I'M AWESOME AND I KNOW IT!
LIST TWO POSITIVE CHARACTERISTICS:

1. _____
2. _____

REFLECTING ON MY FEELING WORD, I WANT TO:

☐ LEVERAGE IT   ☐ CHANGE IT

ONE SMALL ACTION I CAN TAKE TO MOVE FORWARD:

1. _____
_____

NOTES

_____
_____
_____
_____

FINDING MY HAPPY PLACE

It does not matter how slowly you go as long as you do not stop.

– Confucius

DATE _____ FEELING WORD _____

TODAY, I AM GRATEFUL FOR:

1. _____
2. _____
3. _____

I'M AWESOME AND I KNOW IT!
LIST TWO POSITIVE CHARACTERISTICS:

1. _____
2. _____

REFLECTING ON MY FEELING WORD, I WANT TO:

☐ LEVERAGE IT   ☐ CHANGE IT

ONE SMALL ACTION I CAN TAKE TO MOVE FORWARD:

1. _____
   _____

NOTES
_____
_____
_____
_____

FINDING MY HAPPY PLACE

I will love the light for it shows me the way, yet I will endure the darkness because it shows me the stars.

—Og Mandino

DATE _____   FEELING WORD _____

TODAY, I AM GRATEFUL FOR:

1. _____
2. _____
3. _____

I'M AWESOME AND I KNOW IT!
LIST TWO POSITIVE CHARACTERISTICS:

1. _____
2. _____

REFLECTING ON MY FEELING WORD, I WANT TO:

☐ LEVERAGE IT   ☐ CHANGE IT

ONE SMALL ACTION I CAN TAKE TO MOVE FORWARD:

1. _____
   _____

NOTES

_____
_____
_____
_____

FINDING MY HAPPY PLACE

In the middle of difficulty lies opportunity.
—Albert Einstein

DATE _____   FEELING WORD _____

TODAY, I AM GRATEFUL FOR:

1. _____
2. _____
3. _____

I'M AWESOME AND I KNOW IT!
LIST TWO POSITIVE CHARACTERISTICS:

1. _____
2. _____

REFLECTING ON MY FEELING WORD, I WANT TO:

☐ LEVERAGE IT   ☐ CHANGE IT

ONE SMALL ACTION I CAN TAKE TO MOVE FORWARD:

1. _____
   _____

NOTES
_____
_____
_____
_____

FINDING MY HAPPY PLACE

I have not failed. I've just found 10,000 ways that won't work.

-Thomas A. Edison

DATE _____ FEELING WORD _____

TODAY, I AM GRATEFUL FOR:

1. _____
2. _____
3. _____

I'M AWESOME AND I KNOW IT!
LIST TWO POSITIVE CHARACTERISTICS:

1. _____
2. _____

REFLECTING ON MY FEELING WORD, I WANT TO:

☐ LEVERAGE IT   ☐ CHANGE IT

ONE SMALL ACTION I CAN TAKE TO MOVE FORWARD:

1. _____
   _____

NOTES
_____
_____
_____
_____

FINDING MY HAPPY PLACE

Trust because you are willing to accept the risk,
not because it's safe or certain.
-Unknown

DATE _____ FEELING WORD _____

TODAY, I AM GRATEFUL FOR:

1. _____
2. _____
3. _____

I'M AWESOME AND I KNOW IT!
LIST TWO POSITIVE CHARACTERISTICS:

1. _____
2. _____

REFLECTING ON MY FEELING WORD, I WANT TO:

☐ LEVERAGE IT   ☐ CHANGE IT

ONE SMALL ACTION I CAN TAKE TO MOVE FORWARD:

1. _____
   _____

NOTES
_____
_____
_____
_____

FINDING MY HAPPY PLACE

To live a creative life, we must lose our fear of being wrong.

—Joseph Chilton Pearce

DATE _____ FEELING WORD _____

TODAY, I AM GRATEFUL FOR:

1. _____
2. _____
3. _____

I'M AWESOME AND I KNOW IT!
LIST TWO POSITIVE CHARACTERISTICS:

1. _____
2. _____

REFLECTING ON MY FEELING WORD, I WANT TO:

☐ LEVERAGE IT   ☐ CHANGE IT

ONE SMALL ACTION I CAN TAKE TO MOVE FORWARD:

1. _____
   _____

NOTES

_____
_____
_____
_____

FINDING MY HAPPY PLACE

REFLECTION

GRATITUDE SHOULD NOT BE RESERVED FOR
SPECIAL OCCASIONS AND MIRACULOUS
OCCURRENCES.

WHAT WAS LEARNED BY TAKING THE TIME TO
COMPLETE THE FIRST 7 ENTRIES IN THIS
JOURNAL?

_____

_____

_____

_____

_____

_____

_____

_____

_____

_____

_____

_____

_____

_____

_____

_____

_____

_____

FINDING MY HAPPY PLACE

One important key to success is self-confidence. An important key to self-confidence is preparation.

– Arthur Ashe

DATE _____ FEELING WORD _____

TODAY, I AM GRATEFUL FOR:

1._____
2._____
3._____

I'M AWESOME AND I KNOW IT!
LIST TWO POSITIVE CHARACTERISTICS:

1._____
2._____

REFLECTING ON MY FEELING WORD, I WANT TO:

   ☐ LEVERAGE IT   ☐ CHANGE IT

ONE SMALL ACTION I CAN TAKE TO MOVE FORWARD:

1._____
   _____

NOTES
_____
_____
_____
_____

FINDING MY HAPPY PLACE

I don't have any time to stay up all night worrying about what someone who doesn't love me has to say about me.

— Viola Davis

DATE _____ FEELING WORD _____

TODAY, I AM GRATEFUL FOR:

1._____
2._____
3._____

I'M AWESOME AND I KNOW IT!
LIST TWO POSITIVE CHARACTERISTICS:

1._____
2._____

REFLECTING ON MY FEELING WORD, I WANT TO:

☐ LEVERAGE IT   ☐ CHANGE IT

ONE SMALL ACTION I CAN TAKE TO MOVE FORWARD:

1._____
_____

NOTES
_____
_____
_____
_____

FINDING MY HAPPY PLACE

We cannot change the cards we are dealt, just how we play the hand.

— Randy Pausch

DATE _____ FEELING WORD _____

TODAY, I AM GRATEFUL FOR:

1._____
2._____
3._____

I'M AWESOME AND I KNOW IT!
LIST TWO POSITIVE CHARACTERISTICS:

1._____
2._____

REFLECTING ON MY FEELING WORD, I WANT TO:

☐ LEVERAGE IT   ☐ CHANGE IT

ONE SMALL ACTION I CAN TAKE TO MOVE FORWARD:

1._____
_____

NOTES
_____
_____
_____
_____

FINDING MY HAPPY PLACE

There's always something to suggest that you'll never be who you wanted to be. Your choice is to take it or keep on moving.
— Phylicia Rashad

DATE _____ FEELING WORD _____

TODAY, I AM GRATEFUL FOR:

1._____
2._____
3._____

I'M AWESOME AND I KNOW IT!
LIST TWO POSITIVE CHARACTERISTICS:

1._____
2._____

REFLECTING ON MY FEELING WORD, I WANT TO:

☐ LEVERAGE IT   ☐ CHANGE IT

ONE SMALL ACTION I CAN TAKE TO MOVE FORWARD:

1._____
_____

NOTES
_____
_____
_____
_____

FINDING MY HAPPY PLACE

Beginning today, treat everyone you meet as if they were going to be dead by midnight. Extend to them all the care, kindness and understanding you can muster and do it with no thought of any reward. Your life will never be the same again.
- Og Mandino

DATE _____ FEELING WORD _____

TODAY, I AM GRATEFUL FOR:

1._____
2._____
3._____

I'M AWESOME AND I KNOW IT!
LIST TWO POSITIVE CHARACTERISTICS:

1._____
2._____

REFLECTING ON MY FEELING WORD, I WANT TO:

☐ LEVERAGE IT   ☐ CHANGE IT

ONE SMALL ACTION I CAN TAKE TO MOVE FORWARD:

1._____
_____

NOTES
_____
_____
_____
_____

FINDING MY HAPPY PLACE

People often say that motivation doesn't last. Well, neither does bathing — that's why we recommend it daily.
-Zig Ziglar

DATE _____ FEELING WORD _____

TODAY, I AM GRATEFUL FOR:

1._____
2._____
3._____

I'M AWESOME AND I KNOW IT!
LIST TWO POSITIVE CHARACTERISTICS:

1._____
2._____

REFLECTING ON MY FEELING WORD, I WANT TO:

☐ LEVERAGE IT   ☐ CHANGE IT

ONE SMALL ACTION I CAN TAKE TO MOVE FORWARD:

1._____
_____

NOTES
_____
_____
_____
_____

FINDING MY HAPPY PLACE

Do not bring people in your life who weigh you down.
Trust your instincts ... good relationships feel good.
They feel right. They don't hurt. They're not painful.
That's not just with somebody you want to marry,
but it's with the friends that you choose. It's with the
people you surround yourselves with.
— Michelle Obama

DATE _____   FEELING WORD _____

TODAY, I AM GRATEFUL FOR:

1._____
2._____
3._____

I'M AWESOME AND I KNOW IT!
LIST TWO POSITIVE CHARACTERISTICS:

1._____
2._____

REFLECTING ON MY FEELING WORD, I WANT TO:

☐ LEVERAGE IT   ☐ CHANGE IT

ONE SMALL ACTION I CAN TAKE TO MOVE FORWARD:

1._____
_____

NOTES
_____
_____
_____
_____

FINDING MY HAPPY PLACE

A critic is a legless man who teaches running.
- Channing Pollock

DATE _____ FEELING WORD _____

TODAY, I AM GRATEFUL FOR:

1._____
2._____
3._____

I'M AWESOME AND I KNOW IT!
LIST TWO POSITIVE CHARACTERISTICS:

1._____
2._____

REFLECTING ON MY FEELING WORD, I WANT TO:

☐ LEVERAGE IT   ☐ CHANGE IT

ONE SMALL ACTION I CAN TAKE TO MOVE FORWARD:

1._____
_____

NOTES
_____
_____
_____
_____

FINDING MY HAPPY PLACE

This is a wonderful day. I have never seen this one before.

- Maya Angelou

DATE _____ FEELING WORD _____

TODAY, I AM GRATEFUL FOR:

1._____
2._____
3._____

I'M AWESOME AND I KNOW IT!
LIST TWO POSITIVE CHARACTERISTICS:

1._____
2._____

REFLECTING ON MY FEELING WORD, I WANT TO:

☐ LEVERAGE IT   ☐ CHANGE IT

ONE SMALL ACTION I CAN TAKE TO MOVE FORWARD:

1._____
_____

NOTES
_____
_____
_____
_____

FINDING MY HAPPY PLACE

Just when the caterpillar thought the world was ending, he turned into a butterfly.
-Proverb

DATE _____ FEELING WORD _____

TODAY, I AM GRATEFUL FOR:

1._____
2._____
3._____

I'M AWESOME AND I KNOW IT!
LIST TWO POSITIVE CHARACTERISTICS:

1._____
2._____

REFLECTING ON MY FEELING WORD, I WANT TO:

☐ LEVERAGE IT   ☐ CHANGE IT

ONE SMALL ACTION I CAN TAKE TO MOVE FORWARD:

1._____
_____

NOTES
_____
_____
_____
_____

FINDING MY HAPPY PLACE

Sometimes you've got to let everything go – purge yourself. If you are unhappy with anything... whatever is bringing you down, get rid of it. Because you'll find that when you're free, your true creativity, your true self comes out.

– Tina Turner

DATE _____   FEELING WORD _____

TODAY, I AM GRATEFUL FOR:

1._____
2._____
3._____

I'M AWESOME AND I KNOW IT!
LIST TWO POSITIVE CHARACTERISTICS:

1._____
2._____

REFLECTING ON MY FEELING WORD, I WANT TO:

☐ LEVERAGE IT   ☐ CHANGE IT

ONE SMALL ACTION I CAN TAKE TO MOVE FORWARD:

1._____
_____

NOTES
_____
_____
_____
_____

FINDING MY HAPPY PLACE

I believe that the only courage anybody ever needs is the courage to follow your own dreams.
-Oprah Winfrey

MY DREAMS...

_____
_____
_____
_____
_____
_____
_____
_____
_____
_____

WHAT ARE THE BARRIERS BETWEEN MY DREAMS AND MY PRESENT SITUATION?

1. _____
2. _____
3. _____

WHAT AM I GOING TO DO ABOUT THOSE BARRIERS?

1. _____
2. _____
3. _____

FINDING MY HAPPY PLACE

If you don't design your own life plan, chances are you'll fall into someone else's plan. And guess what they have planned for you? Not much.

-Jim Rohn

DATE _____ FEELING WORD _____

TODAY, I AM GRATEFUL FOR:

1._____
2._____
3._____

I'M AWESOME AND I KNOW IT!
LIST TWO POSITIVE CHARACTERISTICS:

1._____
2._____

REFLECTING ON MY FEELING WORD, I WANT TO:

☐ LEVERAGE IT   ☐ CHANGE IT

ONE SMALL ACTION I CAN TAKE TO MOVE FORWARD:

1._____
_____

NOTES

_____
_____
_____
_____

FINDING MY HAPPY PLACE

We all should know that diversity makes for a rich tapestry, and we must understand that all the threads of that tapestry are equal in value no matter their color.

– Maya Angelou

DATE _____ FEELING WORD _____

TODAY, I AM GRATEFUL FOR:

1._____
2._____
3._____

I'M AWESOME AND I KNOW IT!
LIST TWO POSITIVE CHARACTERISTICS:

1._____
2._____

REFLECTING ON MY FEELING WORD, I WANT TO:

☐ LEVERAGE IT   ☐ CHANGE IT

ONE SMALL ACTION I CAN TAKE TO MOVE FORWARD:

1._____
_____

NOTES

_____
_____
_____
_____

FINDING MY HAPPY PLACE

Good, better, best. Never let it rest. 'Till your good is better and your better is best.

- St. Jerome

DATE _____ FEELING WORD _____

TODAY, I AM GRATEFUL FOR:

1._____
2._____
3._____

I'M AWESOME AND I KNOW IT!
LIST TWO POSITIVE CHARACTERISTICS:

1._____
2._____

REFLECTING ON MY FEELING WORD, I WANT TO:

☐ LEVERAGE IT   ☐ CHANGE IT

ONE SMALL ACTION I CAN TAKE TO MOVE FORWARD:

1._____
_____

NOTES
_____
_____
_____
_____

FINDING MY HAPPY PLACE

You are no better than anyone else, and no one is better than you.
– Katherine Johnson

DATE _____ FEELING WORD _____

TODAY, I AM GRATEFUL FOR:

1. _____
2. _____
3. _____

I'M AWESOME AND I KNOW IT!
LIST TWO POSITIVE CHARACTERISTICS:

1. _____
2. _____

REFLECTING ON MY FEELING WORD, I WANT TO:

☐ LEVERAGE IT   ☐ CHANGE IT

ONE SMALL ACTION I CAN TAKE TO MOVE FORWARD:

1. _____
_____

NOTES
_____
_____
_____
_____

FINDING MY HAPPY PLACE

If you want to achieve greatness stop asking for permission.

—Anonymous

DATE _____ FEELING WORD _____

TODAY, I AM GRATEFUL FOR:

1._____
2._____
3._____

I'M AWESOME AND I KNOW IT!
LIST TWO POSITIVE CHARACTERISTICS:

1._____
2._____

REFLECTING ON MY FEELING WORD, I WANT TO:

☐ LEVERAGE IT   ☐ CHANGE IT

ONE SMALL ACTION I CAN TAKE TO MOVE FORWARD:

1._____
_____

NOTES
_____
_____
_____
_____

FINDING MY HAPPY PLACE

Life is not about finding yourself. Life is about creating yourself.

-Lolly Daskal

DATE _____   FEELING WORD _____

TODAY, I AM GRATEFUL FOR:

1._____
2._____
3._____

I'M AWESOME AND I KNOW IT!
LIST TWO POSITIVE CHARACTERISTICS:

1._____
2._____

REFLECTING ON MY FEELING WORD, I WANT TO:

□ LEVERAGE IT   □ CHANGE IT

ONE SMALL ACTION I CAN TAKE TO MOVE FORWARD:

1._____
_____

NOTES
_____
_____
_____
_____

FINDING MY HAPPY PLACE

We must develop and maintain the capacity to forgive. He who is devoid of the power to forgive is devoid of the power to love. There is some good in the worst of us and some evil in the best of us. When we discover this, we are less prone to hate our enemies.

— Martin Luther King, Jr.

DATE _____   FEELING WORD _____

TODAY, I AM GRATEFUL FOR:

1._____
2._____
3._____

I'M AWESOME AND I KNOW IT!
LIST TWO POSITIVE CHARACTERISTICS:

1._____
2._____

REFLECTING ON MY FEELING WORD, I WANT TO:

☐ LEVERAGE IT   ☐ CHANGE IT

ONE SMALL ACTION I CAN TAKE TO MOVE FORWARD:

1._____
_____

NOTES
_____
_____
_____
_____

FINDING MY HAPPY PLACE

Only put off until tomorrow what you are willing to die having left undone.
- Pablo Picasso

DATE _____ FEELING WORD _____

TODAY, I AM GRATEFUL FOR:

1._____
2._____
3._____

I'M AWESOME AND I KNOW IT!
LIST TWO POSITIVE CHARACTERISTICS:

1._____
2._____

REFLECTING ON MY FEELING WORD, I WANT TO:

☐ LEVERAGE IT   ☐ CHANGE IT

ONE SMALL ACTION I CAN TAKE TO MOVE FORWARD:

1._____
_____

NOTES
_____
_____
_____
_____

FINDING MY HAPPY PLACE

Things work out best for those who make the best of how things work out.
—John Wooden

DATE _____   FEELING WORD _____

TODAY, I AM GRATEFUL FOR:

1._____
2._____
3._____

I'M AWESOME AND I KNOW IT!
LIST TWO POSITIVE CHARACTERISTICS:

1._____
2._____

REFLECTING ON MY FEELING WORD, I WANT TO:

☐ LEVERAGE IT   ☐ CHANGE IT

ONE SMALL ACTION I CAN TAKE TO MOVE FORWARD:

1._____
_____

NOTES
_____
_____
_____
_____

FINDING MY HAPPY PLACE

You measure the size of the accomplishment by the obstacles you had to overcome to reach your goals.

– Booker T. Washington

DATE _____   FEELING WORD _____

TODAY, I AM GRATEFUL FOR:

1._____
2._____
3._____

I'M AWESOME AND I KNOW IT!
LIST TWO POSITIVE CHARACTERISTICS:

1._____
2._____

REFLECTING ON MY FEELING WORD, I WANT TO:

☐ LEVERAGE IT   ☐ CHANGE IT

ONE SMALL ACTION I CAN TAKE TO MOVE FORWARD:

1._____
_____

NOTES

_____
_____
_____
_____

FINDING MY HAPPY PLACE

It is not our differences that divide us. It is our inability to recognize, accept, and celebrate those differences.

— Audre Lorde

I'M DIFFERENT IN THE FOLLOWING WAYS:

_____
_____
_____
_____
_____
_____

I'VE CELEBRATED MY DIFFERENCES BY:

_____
_____
_____
_____
_____
_____
_____
_____
_____
_____

FINDING MY HAPPY PLACE

There is no traffic jam along the extra mile.
-Roger Staubach

DATE _____   FEELING WORD _____

TODAY, I AM GRATEFUL FOR:

1. _____
2. _____
3. _____

I'M AWESOME AND I KNOW IT!
LIST TWO POSITIVE CHARACTERISTICS:

1. _____
2. _____

REFLECTING ON MY FEELING WORD, I WANT TO:

☐ LEVERAGE IT   ☐ CHANGE IT

ONE SMALL ACTION I CAN TAKE TO MOVE FORWARD:

1. _____
_____

NOTES
_____
_____
_____
_____

FINDING MY HAPPY PLACE

Success is walking from failure to failure with no loss of enthusiasm.
-Winston Churchill

DATE _____   FEELING WORD _____

TODAY, I AM GRATEFUL FOR:

1._____
2._____
3._____

I'M AWESOME AND I KNOW IT!
LIST TWO POSITIVE CHARACTERISTICS:

1._____
2._____

REFLECTING ON MY FEELING WORD, I WANT TO:

    ☐ LEVERAGE IT   ☐ CHANGE IT

ONE SMALL ACTION I CAN TAKE TO MOVE FORWARD:

1._____

_____

NOTES

_____
_____
_____
_____

FINDING MY HAPPY PLACE

I don't have any time to stay up all night worrying about what someone who doesn't love me has to say about me.

– Viola Davis

DATE _____ FEELING WORD _____

TODAY, I AM GRATEFUL FOR:

1._____
2._____
3._____

I'M AWESOME AND I KNOW IT!
LIST TWO POSITIVE CHARACTERISTICS:

1._____
2._____

REFLECTING ON MY FEELING WORD, I WANT TO:

☐ LEVERAGE IT   ☐ CHANGE IT

ONE SMALL ACTION I CAN TAKE TO MOVE FORWARD:

1._____
_____

NOTES
_____
_____
_____
_____

FINDING MY HAPPY PLACE

Enjoy the little things, for one day you may look back and realize they were the big things.
— Robert Brault

DATE _____ FEELING WORD _____

TODAY, I AM GRATEFUL FOR:

1._____
2._____
3._____

I'M AWESOME AND I KNOW IT!
LIST TWO POSITIVE CHARACTERISTICS:

1._____
2._____

REFLECTING ON MY FEELING WORD, I WANT TO:

☐ LEVERAGE IT   ☐ CHANGE IT

ONE SMALL ACTION I CAN TAKE TO MOVE FORWARD:

1._____
_____

NOTES
_____
_____
_____
_____

If you're walking down the right path and you're willing to keep walking, eventually you'll make progress.

— Barack Obama

DATE _____ FEELING WORD _____

TODAY, I AM GRATEFUL FOR:

1._____
2._____
3._____

I'M AWESOME AND I KNOW IT!
LIST TWO POSITIVE CHARACTERISTICS:

1._____
2._____

REFLECTING ON MY FEELING WORD, I WANT TO:

☐ LEVERAGE IT   ☐ CHANGE IT

ONE SMALL ACTION I CAN TAKE TO MOVE FORWARD:

1._____
_____

NOTES
_____
_____
_____
_____

FINDING MY HAPPY PLACE

You may have to fight a battle more than once to win it.

-Margaret Thatcher

DATE _____   FEELING WORD _____

TODAY, I AM GRATEFUL FOR:

1._____
2._____
3._____

I'M AWESOME AND I KNOW IT!
LIST TWO POSITIVE CHARACTERISTICS:

1._____
2._____

REFLECTING ON MY FEELING WORD, I WANT TO:

☐ LEVERAGE IT   ☐ CHANGE IT

ONE SMALL ACTION I CAN TAKE TO MOVE FORWARD:

1._____
_____

NOTES
_____
_____
_____
_____

FINDING MY HAPPY PLACE

Success is liking yourself, liking what you do, and liking how you do it.
                    -Maya Angelou

DATE _____   FEELING WORD _____

TODAY, I AM GRATEFUL FOR:

1._____
2._____
3._____

I'M AWESOME AND I KNOW IT!
LIST TWO POSITIVE CHARACTERISTICS:

1._____
2._____

REFLECTING ON MY FEELING WORD, I WANT TO:

        ☐ LEVERAGE IT   ☐ CHANGE IT

ONE SMALL ACTION I CAN TAKE TO MOVE FORWARD:

1._____
  _____

NOTES
_____
_____
_____
_____

FINDING MY HAPPY PLACE

Develop success from failures. Discouragement and failure are two of the surest stepping stones to success.
- Dale Carnegie

DATE _____ FEELING WORD _____

TODAY, I AM GRATEFUL FOR:

1._____
2._____
3._____

I'M AWESOME AND I KNOW IT!
LIST TWO POSITIVE CHARACTERISTICS:

1._____
2._____

REFLECTING ON MY FEELING WORD, I WANT TO:

☐ LEVERAGE IT   ☐ CHANGE IT

ONE SMALL ACTION I CAN TAKE TO MOVE FORWARD:

1._____
_____

NOTES
_____
_____
_____
_____

FINDING MY HAPPY PLACE

When it comes to self-care, be more nurturing than necessary.

— Joelle Brake

DATE _____ FEELING WORD _____

TODAY, I AM GRATEFUL FOR:

1._____

2._____

3._____

I'M AWESOME AND I KNOW IT!
LIST TWO POSITIVE CHARACTERISTICS:

1._____

2._____

REFLECTING ON MY FEELING WORD, I WANT TO:

☐ LEVERAGE IT   ☐ CHANGE IT

ONE SMALL ACTION I CAN TAKE TO MOVE FORWARD:

1._____

_____

NOTES
_____
_____
_____
_____

FINDING MY HAPPY PLACE

You have to decide who you are and force the world to deal with you, not with its idea of you.
—James Baldwin

DATE _____ FEELING WORD _____

TODAY, I AM GRATEFUL FOR:

1._____
2._____
3._____

I'M AWESOME AND I KNOW IT!
LIST TWO POSITIVE CHARACTERISTICS:

1._____
2._____

REFLECTING ON MY FEELING WORD, I WANT TO:

☐ LEVERAGE IT   ☐ CHANGE IT

ONE SMALL ACTION I CAN TAKE TO MOVE FORWARD:

1._____
_____

NOTES
_____
_____
_____
_____

FINDING MY HAPPY PLACE

You're not obligated to win. You're obligated to keep trying to do the best you can every day.
— Marian Wright Edelman

DATE _____ FEELING WORD _____

TODAY, I AM GRATEFUL FOR:

1._____
2._____
3._____

I'M AWESOME AND I KNOW IT!
LIST TWO POSITIVE CHARACTERISTICS:

1._____
2._____

REFLECTING ON MY FEELING WORD, I WANT TO:

☐ LEVERAGE IT   ☐ CHANGE IT

ONE SMALL ACTION I CAN TAKE TO MOVE FORWARD:

1._____

_____

NOTES
_____
_____
_____
_____

FINDING MY HAPPY PLACE

I don't want to get to the end of my life and find that I lived just the length of it. I want to have lived the width of it as well.
                    - Diane Ackerman

DATE _____   FEELING WORD _____

TODAY, I AM GRATEFUL FOR:

1._____
2._____
3._____

I'M AWESOME AND I KNOW IT!
LIST TWO POSITIVE CHARACTERISTICS:

1._____
2._____

REFLECTING ON MY FEELING WORD, I WANT TO:

       ☐ LEVERAGE IT   ☐ CHANGE IT

ONE SMALL ACTION I CAN TAKE TO MOVE FORWARD:

1._____
_____

NOTES
_____
_____
_____
_____

FINDING MY HAPPY PLACE

Beginning today, treat everyone you meet as if they were going to be dead by midnight. Extend to them all the care, kindness and understanding you can muster and do it with no thought of any reward. Your life will never be the same again.

- Og Mandino

DATE _____   FEELING WORD _____

TODAY, I AM GRATEFUL FOR:

1._____
2._____
3._____

I'M AWESOME AND I KNOW IT!
LIST TWO POSITIVE CHARACTERISTICS:

1._____
2._____

REFLECTING ON MY FEELING WORD, I WANT TO:

☐ LEVERAGE IT   ☐ CHANGE IT

ONE SMALL ACTION I CAN TAKE TO MOVE FORWARD:

1._____
_____

NOTES
_____
_____
_____
_____

FINDING MY HAPPY PLACE

A successful man is one who can lay a firm foundation with the bricks others have thrown at him.

-David Brinkley

DATE _____   FEELING WORD _____

TODAY, I AM GRATEFUL FOR:

1._____
2._____
3._____

I'M AWESOME AND I KNOW IT!
LIST TWO POSITIVE CHARACTERISTICS:

1._____
2._____

REFLECTING ON MY FEELING WORD, I WANT TO:

☐ LEVERAGE IT   ☐ CHANGE IT

ONE SMALL ACTION I CAN TAKE TO MOVE FORWARD:

1._____
_____

NOTES
_____
_____
_____
_____

FINDING MY HAPPY PLACE

Happiness is a butterfly, which when pursued, is always beyond your grasp, but which, if you will sit down quietly, may alight upon you.
- Nathaniel Hawthorne

DATE _____ FEELING WORD _____

TODAY, I AM GRATEFUL FOR:

1._____
2._____
3._____

I'M AWESOME AND I KNOW IT!
LIST TWO POSITIVE CHARACTERISTICS:

1._____
2._____

REFLECTING ON MY FEELING WORD, I WANT TO:

☐ LEVERAGE IT   ☐ CHANGE IT

ONE SMALL ACTION I CAN TAKE TO MOVE FORWARD:

1._____
_____

NOTES
_____
_____
_____
_____

FINDING MY HAPPY PLACE

Trade your expectations for appreciation and your world changes instantly.
— Tony Robbins

YOU'RE ABOUT HALFWAY ALONG IN YOUR GRATITUDE JOURNAL.

GRATITUDE
- OPENS THE DOOR TO MORE RELATIONSHIPS
- IMPROVES PSYCHOLOGICAL HEALTH
- IMPROVES SELF-ESTEEM

LIST 5 THINGS YOU APPRECIATE, BUT OFTEN TAKE FOR GRANTED:

1._____
2._____
3._____
4._____
5._____

LIST 3 PEOPLE TO CONTACT TODAY BECAUSE YOU WANT TO EXPRESS YOUR APPRECIATION:

1._____
2._____
3._____

FINDING MY HAPPY PLACE

To conquer oneself is a greater victory than to conquer thousands in a battle.
– Dalai Lama

DATE _____ FEELING WORD _____

TODAY, I AM GRATEFUL FOR:

1. _____
2. _____
3. _____

I'M AWESOME AND I KNOW IT!
LIST TWO POSITIVE CHARACTERISTICS:

1. _____
2. _____

REFLECTING ON MY FEELING WORD, I WANT TO:

☐ LEVERAGE IT   ☐ CHANGE IT

ONE SMALL ACTION I CAN TAKE TO MOVE FORWARD:

1. _____
   _____

NOTES

_____
_____
_____
_____

FINDING MY HAPPY PLACE

Do your little bit of good where you are; it's those little bits of good put together that overwhelm the world.

— Desmond Tutu

DATE _____ FEELING WORD _____

TODAY, I AM GRATEFUL FOR:

1._____
2._____
3._____

I'M AWESOME AND I KNOW IT!
LIST TWO POSITIVE CHARACTERISTICS:

1._____
2._____

REFLECTING ON MY FEELING WORD, I WANT TO:

☐ LEVERAGE IT   ☐ CHANGE IT

ONE SMALL ACTION I CAN TAKE TO MOVE FORWARD:

1._____
_____

NOTES
_____
_____
_____
_____

FINDING MY HAPPY PLACE

It's not what you look at that matters, it's what you see.

- Anonymous

DATE _____ FEELING WORD _____

TODAY, I AM GRATEFUL FOR:

1._____
2._____
3._____

I'M AWESOME AND I KNOW IT!
LIST TWO POSITIVE CHARACTERISTICS:

1._____
2._____

REFLECTING ON MY FEELING WORD, I WANT TO:

☐ LEVERAGE IT   ☐ CHANGE IT

ONE SMALL ACTION I CAN TAKE TO MOVE FORWARD:

1._____
   _____

NOTES
_____
_____
_____
_____

FINDING MY HAPPY PLACE

Do things that make you happy within the confines of the legal system.
— Ellen DeGeneres

DATE _____   FEELING WORD _____

TODAY, I AM GRATEFUL FOR:

1._____
2._____
3._____

I'M AWESOME AND I KNOW IT!
LIST TWO POSITIVE CHARACTERISTICS:

1._____
2._____

REFLECTING ON MY FEELING WORD, I WANT TO:

☐ LEVERAGE IT   ☐ CHANGE IT

ONE SMALL ACTION I CAN TAKE TO MOVE FORWARD:

1._____
_____

NOTES

_____
_____
_____
_____

FINDING MY HAPPY PLACE

Change will not come if we wait for some other person or some other time. We are the ones we've been waiting for. We are the change that we seek.
— Barack Obama

DATE _____ FEELING WORD _____

TODAY, I AM GRATEFUL FOR:

1._____
2._____
3._____

I'M AWESOME AND I KNOW IT!
LIST TWO POSITIVE CHARACTERISTICS:

1._____
2._____

REFLECTING ON MY FEELING WORD, I WANT TO:

☐ LEVERAGE IT   ☐ CHANGE IT

ONE SMALL ACTION I CAN TAKE TO MOVE FORWARD:

1._____
_____

NOTES
_____
_____
_____
_____

FINDING MY HAPPY PLACE

You never know which experiences of life are going to be of value . . . You've got to leave yourself open to the hidden opportunities.
– Robin Roberts

DATE _____ FEELING WORD _____

TODAY, I AM GRATEFUL FOR:

1._____

2._____

3._____

I'M AWESOME AND I KNOW IT!
LIST TWO POSITIVE CHARACTERISTICS:

1._____

2._____

REFLECTING ON MY FEELING WORD, I WANT TO:

☐ LEVERAGE IT   ☐ CHANGE IT

ONE SMALL ACTION I CAN TAKE TO MOVE FORWARD:

1._____

_____

NOTES

_____
_____
_____
_____

FINDING MY HAPPY PLACE

The obscure we see eventually. The completely apparent takes even longer.

- Edward R. Murrow

DATE _____ FEELING WORD _____

TODAY, I AM GRATEFUL FOR:

1._____
2._____
3._____

I'M AWESOME AND I KNOW IT!
LIST TWO POSITIVE CHARACTERISTICS:

1._____
2._____

REFLECTING ON MY FEELING WORD, I WANT TO:

☐ LEVERAGE IT   ☐ CHANGE IT

ONE SMALL ACTION I CAN TAKE TO MOVE FORWARD:

1._____
_____

NOTES
_____
_____
_____
_____

FINDING MY HAPPY PLACE

When your job begins to compromise your health, a change is necessary - either change what's causing the problem or change your job.
- Joelle Brake

DATE _____ FEELING WORD _____

TODAY, I AM GRATEFUL FOR:

1._____
2._____
3._____

I'M AWESOME AND I KNOW IT!
LIST TWO POSITIVE CHARACTERISTICS:

1._____
2._____

REFLECTING ON MY FEELING WORD, I WANT TO:

☐ LEVERAGE IT   ☐ CHANGE IT

ONE SMALL ACTION I CAN TAKE TO MOVE FORWARD:

1._____
_____

NOTES
_____
_____
_____
_____

FINDING MY HAPPY PLACE

Start where you are. Use what you have. Do what you can.

– Arthur Ashe

DATE _____ FEELING WORD _____

TODAY, I AM GRATEFUL FOR:

1._____
2._____
3._____

I'M AWESOME AND I KNOW IT!
LIST TWO POSITIVE CHARACTERISTICS:

1._____
2._____

REFLECTING ON MY FEELING WORD, I WANT TO:

    □ LEVERAGE IT   □ CHANGE IT

ONE SMALL ACTION I CAN TAKE TO MOVE FORWARD:

1._____
  _____

NOTES
_____
_____
_____
_____

FINDING MY HAPPY PLACE

It is failure that gives you the proper perspective on success.

— Ellen DeGeneres

DATE _____ FEELING WORD _____

TODAY, I AM GRATEFUL FOR:

1._____
2._____
3._____

I'M AWESOME AND I KNOW IT!
LIST TWO POSITIVE CHARACTERISTICS:

1._____
2._____

REFLECTING ON MY FEELING WORD, I WANT TO:

☐ LEVERAGE IT   ☐ CHANGE IT

ONE SMALL ACTION I CAN TAKE TO MOVE FORWARD:

1._____
_____

NOTES
_____
_____
_____
_____

FINDING MY HAPPY PLACE

The roots of all goodness lie in the soil of appreciation for goodness.
— Dalai Lama

DATE _____ FEELING WORD _____

TODAY, I AM GRATEFUL FOR:

1._____
2._____
3._____

I'M AWESOME AND I KNOW IT!
LIST TWO POSITIVE CHARACTERISTICS:

1._____
2._____

REFLECTING ON MY FEELING WORD, I WANT TO:

☐ LEVERAGE IT   ☐ CHANGE IT

ONE SMALL ACTION I CAN TAKE TO MOVE FORWARD:

1._____
_____

NOTES
_____
_____
_____
_____

FINDING MY HAPPY PLACE

Hope is being able to see that there is light despite all of the darkness.

— Desmond Tutu

DATE _____ FEELING WORD _____

TODAY, I AM GRATEFUL FOR:

1._____
2._____
3._____

I'M AWESOME AND I KNOW IT!
LIST TWO POSITIVE CHARACTERISTICS:

1._____
2._____

REFLECTING ON MY FEELING WORD, I WANT TO:

☐ LEVERAGE IT   ☐ CHANGE IT

ONE SMALL ACTION I CAN TAKE TO MOVE FORWARD:

1._____
_____

NOTES
_____
_____
_____
_____

FINDING MY HAPPY PLACE

Not everything that is faced can be changed, but nothing can be changed until it is faced.
— James Baldwin

DATE _____   FEELING WORD _____

TODAY, I AM GRATEFUL FOR:

1. _____
2. _____
3. _____

I'M AWESOME AND I KNOW IT!
LIST TWO POSITIVE CHARACTERISTICS:

1. _____
2. _____

REFLECTING ON MY FEELING WORD, I WANT TO:

☐ LEVERAGE IT   ☐ CHANGE IT

ONE SMALL ACTION I CAN TAKE TO MOVE FORWARD:

1. _____
   _____

NOTES
_____
_____
_____
_____

FINDING MY HAPPY PLACE

We may stumble and fall but shall rise again; it should be enough if we did not run away from the battle.

– Mahatma Gandhi

DATE _____ FEELING WORD _____

TODAY, I AM GRATEFUL FOR:

1._____
2._____
3._____

I'M AWESOME AND I KNOW IT!
LIST TWO POSITIVE CHARACTERISTICS:

1._____
2._____

REFLECTING ON MY FEELING WORD, I WANT TO:

☐ LEVERAGE IT   ☐ CHANGE IT

ONE SMALL ACTION I CAN TAKE TO MOVE FORWARD:

1._____
_____

NOTES

_____
_____
_____
_____

FINDING MY HAPPY PLACE

A diamond is merely a lump of coal that did well under pressure.

— Unknown

DATE _____ FEELING WORD _____

TODAY, I AM GRATEFUL FOR:

1._____
2._____
3._____

I'M AWESOME AND I KNOW IT!
LIST TWO POSITIVE CHARACTERISTICS:

1._____
2._____

REFLECTING ON MY FEELING WORD, I WANT TO:

☐ LEVERAGE IT   ☐ CHANGE IT

ONE SMALL ACTION I CAN TAKE TO MOVE FORWARD:

1._____
_____

NOTES
_____
_____
_____
_____

FINDING MY HAPPY PLACE

You're only given a little spark of madness. You mustn't lose it.

– Robin Williams

DATE _____ FEELING WORD _____

TODAY, I AM GRATEFUL FOR:

1._____
2._____
3._____

I'M AWESOME AND I KNOW IT!
LIST TWO POSITIVE CHARACTERISTICS:

1._____
2._____

REFLECTING ON MY FEELING WORD, I WANT TO:

☐ LEVERAGE IT   ☐ CHANGE IT

ONE SMALL ACTION I CAN TAKE TO MOVE FORWARD:

1._____

_____

NOTES
_____
_____
_____
_____

FINDING MY HAPPY PLACE

Optimist: someone who figures that taking a step backward after taking a step forward is not a disaster, it's more like a cha-cha.

— Robert Brault

DATE _____   FEELING WORD _____

TODAY, I AM GRATEFUL FOR:

1._____
2._____
3._____

I'M AWESOME AND I KNOW IT!
LIST TWO POSITIVE CHARACTERISTICS:

1._____
2._____

REFLECTING ON MY FEELING WORD, I WANT TO:

☐ LEVERAGE IT   ☐ CHANGE IT

ONE SMALL ACTION I CAN TAKE TO MOVE FORWARD:

1._____
_____

NOTES

_____
_____
_____
_____

FINDING MY HAPPY PLACE

Think like a proton. Always positive.
– Unknown

DATE _____ FEELING WORD _____

TODAY, I AM GRATEFUL FOR:

1._____
2._____
3._____

I'M AWESOME AND I KNOW IT!
LIST TWO POSITIVE CHARACTERISTICS:

1._____
2._____

REFLECTING ON MY FEELING WORD, I WANT TO:

☐ LEVERAGE IT   ☐ CHANGE IT

ONE SMALL ACTION I CAN TAKE TO MOVE FORWARD:

1._____
_____

NOTES
_____
_____
_____
_____

FINDING MY HAPPY PLACE

The elevator to success is out of order. You'll have to use the stairs, one step at a time.
— Joe Girard

DATE _____ FEELING WORD _____

TODAY, I AM GRATEFUL FOR:

1. _____
2. _____
3. _____

I'M AWESOME AND I KNOW IT!
LIST TWO POSITIVE CHARACTERISTICS:

1. _____
2. _____

REFLECTING ON MY FEELING WORD, I WANT TO:

☐ LEVERAGE IT   ☐ CHANGE IT

ONE SMALL ACTION I CAN TAKE TO MOVE FORWARD:

1. _____
_____

NOTES
_____
_____
_____
_____

FINDING MY HAPPY PLACE

It's our challenges and obstacles that give us layers of depth and make us interesting. Are they fun when they happen? No. But they are what make us unique.
  – Ellen DeGeneres

DATE _____   FEELING WORD _____

TODAY, I AM GRATEFUL FOR:

1._____
2._____
3._____

I'M AWESOME AND I KNOW IT!
LIST TWO POSITIVE CHARACTERISTICS:

1._____
2._____

REFLECTING ON MY FEELING WORD, I WANT TO:

☐ LEVERAGE IT   ☐ CHANGE IT

ONE SMALL ACTION I CAN TAKE TO MOVE FORWARD:

1._____
_____

NOTES
_____
_____
_____
_____

FINDING MY HAPPY PLACE

As we express our gratitude, we must never forget that the highest appreciation is not to utter words but to live by them.

—John F. Kennedy

DATE _____ FEELING WORD _____

TODAY, I AM GRATEFUL FOR:

1. _____
2. _____
3. _____

I'M AWESOME AND I KNOW IT!
LIST TWO POSITIVE CHARACTERISTICS:

1. _____
2. _____

REFLECTING ON MY FEELING WORD, I WANT TO:

☐ LEVERAGE IT   ☐ CHANGE IT

ONE SMALL ACTION I CAN TAKE TO MOVE FORWARD:

1. _____
_____

NOTES
_____
_____
_____
_____

FINDING MY HAPPY PLACE

At times, our own light goes out and is rekindled by a spark from another person. Each of us has cause to think with deep gratitude of those who have lighted the flame within us.
– Albert Schweitzer

DATE _____   FEELING WORD _____

TODAY, I AM GRATEFUL FOR:

1. _____
2. _____
3. _____

I'M AWESOME AND I KNOW IT!
LIST TWO POSITIVE CHARACTERISTICS:

1. _____
2. _____

REFLECTING ON MY FEELING WORD, I WANT TO:

☐ LEVERAGE IT   ☐ CHANGE IT

ONE SMALL ACTION I CAN TAKE TO MOVE FORWARD:

1. _____
_____

NOTES

_____
_____
_____
_____

FINDING MY HAPPY PLACE

One of the lessons that I grew up with was to always stay true to yourself and never let what somebody else says distract you from your goals. And so when I hear about negative and false attacks, I really don't invest any energy in them, because I know who I am.

— Michelle Obama

DATE _____ FEELING WORD _____

TODAY, I AM GRATEFUL FOR:

1._____
2._____
3._____

I'M AWESOME AND I KNOW IT!
LIST TWO POSITIVE CHARACTERISTICS:

1._____
2._____

REFLECTING ON MY FEELING WORD, I WANT TO:

☐ LEVERAGE IT   ☐ CHANGE IT

ONE SMALL ACTION I CAN TAKE TO MOVE FORWARD:

1._____
_____

NOTES
_____
_____
_____
_____

FINDING MY HAPPY PLACE

*If you don't like something, change it. If you
can't change it, change your attitude.*
— Maya Angelou

DATE _____   FEELING WORD _____

TODAY, I AM GRATEFUL FOR:

1._____
2._____
3._____

I'M AWESOME AND I KNOW IT!
LIST TWO POSITIVE CHARACTERISTICS:

1._____
2._____

REFLECTING ON MY FEELING WORD, I WANT TO:

☐ LEVERAGE IT   ☐ CHANGE IT

ONE SMALL ACTION I CAN TAKE TO MOVE FORWARD:

1._____
_____

NOTES
_____
_____
_____
_____

FINDING MY HAPPY PLACE

Never be limited by other people's limited imaginations. If you adopt their attitudes, then the possibility won't exist because you'll have already shut it out...You can hear other people's wisdom, but you've got to re-evaluate the world for yourself.

– Dr. Mae Jemison

DATE _____ FEELING WORD _____

TODAY, I AM GRATEFUL FOR:

1._____
2._____
3._____

I'M AWESOME AND I KNOW IT!
LIST TWO POSITIVE CHARACTERISTICS:

1._____
2._____

REFLECTING ON MY FEELING WORD, I WANT TO:

☐ LEVERAGE IT   ☐ CHANGE IT

ONE SMALL ACTION I CAN TAKE TO MOVE FORWARD:

1._____
_____

NOTES
_____
_____
_____
_____

FINDING MY HAPPY PLACE

I used to think I was indecisive, but now I'm not so sure.

— Unknown

DATE _____   FEELING WORD _____

TODAY, I AM GRATEFUL FOR:

1._____
2._____
3._____

I'M AWESOME AND I KNOW IT!
LIST TWO POSITIVE CHARACTERISTICS:

1._____
2._____

REFLECTING ON MY FEELING WORD, I WANT TO:

☐ LEVERAGE IT   ☐ CHANGE IT

ONE SMALL ACTION I CAN TAKE TO MOVE FORWARD:

1._____

_____

NOTES
_____
_____
_____
_____

FINDING MY HAPPY PLACE

Anger and hatred are signs of weakness, while compassion is a sure sign of strength.
– Dalai Lama

DATE _____ FEELING WORD _____

TODAY, I AM GRATEFUL FOR:

1._____
2._____
3._____

I'M AWESOME AND I KNOW IT!
LIST TWO POSITIVE CHARACTERISTICS:

1._____
2._____

REFLECTING ON MY FEELING WORD, I WANT TO:

☐ LEVERAGE IT   ☐ CHANGE IT

ONE SMALL ACTION I CAN TAKE TO MOVE FORWARD:

1._____
_____

NOTES
_____
_____
_____
_____

FINDING MY HAPPY PLACE

*Courage is resistance to fear, mastery of fear--
not absence of fear.*
        - Mark Twain

DATE _____   FEELING WORD _____

TODAY, I AM GRATEFUL FOR:

1._____
2._____
3._____

I'M AWESOME AND I KNOW IT!
LIST TWO POSITIVE CHARACTERISTICS:

1._____
2._____

REFLECTING ON MY FEELING WORD, I WANT TO:

    ☐ LEVERAGE IT   ☐ CHANGE IT

ONE SMALL ACTION I CAN TAKE TO MOVE FORWARD:

1._____

_____

NOTES
_____
_____
_____
_____

FINDING MY HAPPY PLACE

The secret of health for both mind and body is not to mourn for the past, not to worry about the future, but to live the present moment wisely and earnestly.

−Buddha

DATE _____ FEELING WORD _____

TODAY, I AM GRATEFUL FOR:

1._____
2._____
3._____

I'M AWESOME AND I KNOW IT!
LIST TWO POSITIVE CHARACTERISTICS:

1._____
2._____

REFLECTING ON MY FEELING WORD, I WANT TO:

☐ LEVERAGE IT   ☐ CHANGE IT

ONE SMALL ACTION I CAN TAKE TO MOVE FORWARD:

1._____
_____

NOTES
_____
_____
_____
_____

FINDING MY HAPPY PLACE

And you ask 'What if I fall?' Oh but my darling, what if you fly?

—Erin Hanson

DATE _____   FEELING WORD _____

TODAY, I AM GRATEFUL FOR:

1._____
2._____
3._____

I'M AWESOME AND I KNOW IT!
LIST TWO POSITIVE CHARACTERISTICS:

1._____
2._____

REFLECTING ON MY FEELING WORD, I WANT TO:

☐ LEVERAGE IT   ☐ CHANGE IT

ONE SMALL ACTION I CAN TAKE TO MOVE FORWARD:

1._____

_____

NOTES
_____
_____
_____
_____

FINDING MY HAPPY PLACE

Embrace uncertainty. Some of the most beautiful chapters in our lives won't have a title until much later.

−Bob Goff

DATE _____ FEELING WORD _____

TODAY, I AM GRATEFUL FOR:

1._____
2._____
3._____

I'M AWESOME AND I KNOW IT!
LIST TWO POSITIVE CHARACTERISTICS:

1._____
2._____

REFLECTING ON MY FEELING WORD, I WANT TO:

☐ LEVERAGE IT   ☐ CHANGE IT

ONE SMALL ACTION I CAN TAKE TO MOVE FORWARD:

1._____
_____

NOTES
_____
_____
_____
_____

FINDING MY HAPPY PLACE

No one can make you feel inferior without your consent.

- Eleanor Roosevelt

"A SNUB" DEFINED THE FIRST LADY, "IS THE EFFORT OF A PERSON WHO FEELS SUPERIOR TO MAKE SOMEONE ELSE FEEL INFERIOR. TO DO SO, HE HAS TO FIND SOMEONE WHO CAN BE MADE TO FEEL INFERIOR."

HAS ANYONE TRIED TO SNUB YOU OR INFLUENCE YOUR THOUGHTS TOWARDS INFERIORITY?

I FELT SNUBBED WHEN:

_____

_____

_____

_____

I RESPONDED BY:

_____

_____

_____

_____

AN ATTITUDE OF GRATITUDE LEADS TO HAPPINESS, AND THIS CAN EQUIP YOU WITH THE LEVEL OF RESILIENCE NECESSARY TO REJECT THOUGHTS OF INTERNALIZING A SNUB.

FINDING MY HAPPY PLACE

Don't let a bad situation bring out the worst in you. Before you respond, breathe deeply and ask yourself what possible good could come of this.
— Joelle Brake

DATE _____   FEELING WORD _____

TODAY, I AM GRATEFUL FOR:

1._____
2._____
3._____

I'M AWESOME AND I KNOW IT!
LIST TWO POSITIVE CHARACTERISTICS:

1._____
2._____

REFLECTING ON MY FEELING WORD, I WANT TO:

    ☐ LEVERAGE IT   ☐ CHANGE IT

ONE SMALL ACTION I CAN TAKE TO MOVE FORWARD:

1._____
_____

NOTES
_____
_____
_____
_____

FINDING MY HAPPY PLACE

At the center of your being you have the answer; you know who you are and you know what you want.

– Lao Tzu

DATE _____ FEELING WORD _____

TODAY, I AM GRATEFUL FOR:

1._____
2._____
3._____

I'M AWESOME AND I KNOW IT!
LIST TWO POSITIVE CHARACTERISTICS:

1._____
2._____

REFLECTING ON MY FEELING WORD, I WANT TO:

☐ LEVERAGE IT   ☐ CHANGE IT

ONE SMALL ACTION I CAN TAKE TO MOVE FORWARD:

1._____
_____

NOTES

_____
_____
_____
_____

FINDING MY HAPPY PLACE

The splendid thing about falling apart silently... is that you can start over as many times as you like.
  – Sanober Khan, A Thousand Flamingos

DATE _____   FEELING WORD _____

TODAY, I AM GRATEFUL FOR:

1._____
2._____
3._____

I'M AWESOME AND I KNOW IT!
LIST TWO POSITIVE CHARACTERISTICS:

1._____
2._____

REFLECTING ON MY FEELING WORD, I WANT TO:

      ☐ LEVERAGE IT   ☐ CHANGE IT

ONE SMALL ACTION I CAN TAKE TO MOVE FORWARD:

1._____
_____

NOTES
_____
_____
_____
_____

FINDING MY HAPPY PLACE

Forgiveness means letting go of the hope for a better past.

– Lama Surya Das

DATE _____ FEELING WORD _____

TODAY, I AM GRATEFUL FOR:

1._____
2._____
3._____

I'M AWESOME AND I KNOW IT!
LIST TWO POSITIVE CHARACTERISTICS:

1._____
2._____

REFLECTING ON MY FEELING WORD, I WANT TO:

☐ LEVERAGE IT   ☐ CHANGE IT

ONE SMALL ACTION I CAN TAKE TO MOVE FORWARD:

1._____

_____

NOTES
_____
_____
_____
_____

FINDING MY HAPPY PLACE

Thank you is the best prayer that anyone could say. I say that one a lot. Thank you expresses extreme gratitude, humility and understanding.
— Alice Walker

DATE _____   FEELING WORD _____

TODAY, I AM GRATEFUL FOR:

1._____
2._____
3._____

I'M AWESOME AND I KNOW IT!
LIST TWO POSITIVE CHARACTERISTICS:

1._____
2._____

REFLECTING ON MY FEELING WORD, I WANT TO:

☐ LEVERAGE IT   ☐ CHANGE IT

ONE SMALL ACTION I CAN TAKE TO MOVE FORWARD:

1._____
_____

NOTES
_____
_____
_____
_____

FINDING MY HAPPY PLACE

The hardest arithmetic to master is that which enables us to count our blessings
— Eric Hoffer

DATE _____ FEELING WORD _____

TODAY, I AM GRATEFUL FOR:

1._____
2._____
3._____

I'M AWESOME AND I KNOW IT!
LIST TWO POSITIVE CHARACTERISTICS:

1._____
2._____

REFLECTING ON MY FEELING WORD, I WANT TO:

☐ LEVERAGE IT   ☐ CHANGE IT

ONE SMALL ACTION I CAN TAKE TO MOVE FORWARD:

1._____
_____

NOTES
_____
_____
_____
_____

FINDING MY HAPPY PLACE

Gratitude can transform common days into thanksgivings, turn routine jobs into joy, and change ordinary opportunities into blessings.
– William Arthur Ward

DATE _____ FEELING WORD _____

TODAY, I AM GRATEFUL FOR:

1._____
2._____
3._____

I'M AWESOME AND I KNOW IT!
LIST TWO POSITIVE CHARACTERISTICS:

1._____
2._____

REFLECTING ON MY FEELING WORD, I WANT TO:

☐ LEVERAGE IT   ☐ CHANGE IT

ONE SMALL ACTION I CAN TAKE TO MOVE FORWARD:

1._____
_____

NOTES
_____
_____
_____
_____

FINDING MY HAPPY PLACE

Thankfulness is the beginning of gratitude.
Gratitude is the completion of thankfulness.
Thankfulness may consist merely in words.
Gratitude is shown is acts.
- Henri Frederic Amiel

DATE _____   FEELING WORD _____

TODAY, I AM GRATEFUL FOR:

1._____
2._____
3._____

I'M AWESOME AND I KNOW IT!
LIST TWO POSITIVE CHARACTERISTICS:

1._____
2._____

REFLECTING ON MY FEELING WORD, I WANT TO:

☐ LEVERAGE IT   ☐ CHANGE IT

ONE SMALL ACTION I CAN TAKE TO MOVE FORWARD:

1._____
_____

NOTES

_____
_____
_____
_____

FINDING MY HAPPY PLACE

Gratitude bestows reverence, allowing us to encounter everyday epiphanies, those transcendent moments of awe that change forever how we experience life and the world.

— John Milton

DATE _____ FEELING WORD _____

TODAY, I AM GRATEFUL FOR:

1._____
2._____
3._____

I'M AWESOME AND I KNOW IT!
LIST TWO POSITIVE CHARACTERISTICS:

1._____
2._____

REFLECTING ON MY FEELING WORD, I WANT TO:

□ LEVERAGE IT   □ CHANGE IT

ONE SMALL ACTION I CAN TAKE TO MOVE FORWARD:

1._____
_____

NOTES

_____
_____
_____
_____

FINDING MY HAPPY PLACE

It is not happy people who are thankful, it is thankful people who are happy.
– Unknown

DATE _____ FEELING WORD _____

TODAY, I AM GRATEFUL FOR:

1._____
2._____
3._____

I'M AWESOME AND I KNOW IT!
LIST TWO POSITIVE CHARACTERISTICS:

1._____
2._____

REFLECTING ON MY FEELING WORD, I WANT TO:

☐ LEVERAGE IT   ☐ CHANGE IT

ONE SMALL ACTION I CAN TAKE TO MOVE FORWARD:

1._____
_____

NOTES
_____
_____
_____
_____

FINDING MY HAPPY PLACE

Gratitude unlocks the fullness of life. It turns what we have into enough, and more. It turns denial into acceptance, chaos into order, confusion into clarity. It turns problems into gifts, failures into success, the unexpected into perfect timing, and mistakes into important events.

- Melodie Beattie

DATE _____ FEELING WORD _____

TODAY, I AM GRATEFUL FOR:

1._____
2._____
3._____

I'M AWESOME AND I KNOW IT!
LIST TWO POSITIVE CHARACTERISTICS:

1._____
2._____

REFLECTING ON MY FEELING WORD, I WANT TO:

☐ LEVERAGE IT   ☐ CHANGE IT

ONE SMALL ACTION I CAN TAKE TO MOVE FORWARD:

1._____
_____

NOTES

_____
_____
_____
_____

FINDING MY HAPPY PLACE

Reflect upon your present blessings, for which every man has plenty; not on your past misfortunes, of which all men have some.
— Charles Dickens

DATE _____ FEELING WORD _____

TODAY, I AM GRATEFUL FOR:

1._____
2._____
3._____

I'M AWESOME AND I KNOW IT!
LIST TWO POSITIVE CHARACTERISTICS:

1._____
2._____

REFLECTING ON MY FEELING WORD, I WANT TO:

☐ LEVERAGE IT ☐ CHANGE IT

ONE SMALL ACTION I CAN TAKE TO MOVE FORWARD:

1._____
_____

NOTES
_____
_____
_____
_____

FINDING MY HAPPY PLACE

You pray for rain, you gotta deal with the mud too. That's a part of it.
— Denzel Washington

DATE _____ FEELING WORD _____

TODAY, I AM GRATEFUL FOR:

1._____
2._____
3._____

I'M AWESOME AND I KNOW IT!
LIST TWO POSITIVE CHARACTERISTICS:

1._____
2._____

REFLECTING ON MY FEELING WORD, I WANT TO:

☐ LEVERAGE IT   ☐ CHANGE IT

ONE SMALL ACTION I CAN TAKE TO MOVE FORWARD:

1._____
_____

NOTES
_____
_____
_____
_____

FINDING MY HAPPY PLACE

Don't be afraid of failure. This is the way to succeed.

— LeBron James

DATE _____ FEELING WORD _____

TODAY, I AM GRATEFUL FOR:

1._____
2._____
3._____

I'M AWESOME AND I KNOW IT!
LIST TWO POSITIVE CHARACTERISTICS:

1._____
2._____

REFLECTING ON MY FEELING WORD, I WANT TO:

☐ LEVERAGE IT   ☐ CHANGE IT

ONE SMALL ACTION I CAN TAKE TO MOVE FORWARD:

1._____
_____

NOTES

_____
_____
_____
_____

FINDING MY HAPPY PLACE

If you look at what you have in life, you'll always have more. If you look at what you don't have in life, you'll never have enough.
— Oprah Winfrey

DATE _____ FEELING WORD _____

TODAY, I AM GRATEFUL FOR:

1._____
2._____
3._____

I'M AWESOME AND I KNOW IT!
LIST TWO POSITIVE CHARACTERISTICS:

1._____
2._____

REFLECTING ON MY FEELING WORD, I WANT TO:

☐ LEVERAGE IT   ☐ CHANGE IT

ONE SMALL ACTION I CAN TAKE TO MOVE FORWARD:

1._____
_____

NOTES
_____
_____
_____
_____

FINDING MY HAPPY PLACE

Remember to take care of yourself. You can't pour from an empty cup.
- Unknown

DATE _____   FEELING WORD _____

TODAY, I AM GRATEFUL FOR:

1._____
2._____
3._____

I'M AWESOME AND I KNOW IT!
LIST TWO POSITIVE CHARACTERISTICS:

1._____
2._____

REFLECTING ON MY FEELING WORD, I WANT TO:

☐ LEVERAGE IT   ☐ CHANGE IT

ONE SMALL ACTION I CAN TAKE TO MOVE FORWARD:

1._____
_____

NOTES
_____
_____
_____
_____

FINDING MY HAPPY PLACE

REFLECTION

_____
_____
_____
_____
_____
_____
_____
_____
_____
_____
_____
_____
_____
_____
_____
_____
_____
_____

FINDING MY HAPPY PLACE

Perhaps I'm not there yet, but I'm closer than I was *yesterday.*

An attitude of gratitude leads to happiness.

FINDING MY HAPPY PLACE

Dedication

My high school English teacher gifted me with my first journal when I set off for college. That journal got me through some tough times. She told me about the benefits of putting your thoughts down on paper.

I dedicate this journal to my loving husband, who has been overwhelmingly supportive throughout my journey, my amazing daughters who are gentle yet fierce, my family & friends who have listened without judgment and somehow always find a way to make me laugh, and my high school English teacher who introduced me to journaling. I thank you all.

When I transitioned to a gratitude journal, one of the first entries expressed a deep appreciation for my therapist, Hillary Schultz, M.Ed., PCC,-s. With my very high expectations of myself, she taught me to be kind to myself and frequently told me, "you are what you think." She taught me that putting others first shows them who's second.

Mental health is as important as physical health. Hillary was my fourth therapist. I just didn't gel with the others. With that said, if you have tried therapy and it didn't work out, try a different therapist. Keep trying until you get the help you need.

Take care of yourself. Remember, an attitude of gratitude leads to happiness. You can't pour from an empty cup.

Thank You,

Joelle

FINDING MY HAPPY PLACE

Feeling Words & Emotions

It can be difficult to find a word to describe how you're feeling, but feelings can be confusing. Don't worry, this level of emotional confusion is actually pretty common.

Feelings and emotions are ever-changing, and while it is important to learn the skills to identify your feelings, it's equally important to focus on how you're going to react to them. Decide if you want to leverage the feeling and build upon it or if you want to change the feeling.

Take a look at the suggestions below:

Assertive
Confident
Determined
Important
Powerful
Proud
Respected
Successful
Sure
Valued
Worthwhile
Bold
Brave

Amused
Creative
Curious
Daring
Ecstatic
Energetic
Enthusiastic
Excited
Happy
Hopeful
Loved
Lovestruck
Mischievous
Optimistic

Anxious
Bewildered
Confused
Discouraged
Embarrassed
Helpless
Humiliated
Hysterical
Inadequate
Insecure
Insignificant
Pained
Paranoid
Rejected
Scared
Submissive
Withdrawn

Aggressive
Angry
Annoyed
Bitter
Disgusted
Envious
Frustrated
Hurt
Cranky
Mad
Selfish

Skeptical
Stubborn

Alienated
Apathetic
Ashamed
Bored
Depressed
Disappointed
Exhausted
Guilty
Inferior
Lonely
Miserable
Regretful
Remorseful
Sad
Stupid

Appreciative
Content
Relaxed
Relieved
Humbled
Secure
Forgiving
Nurturing
Peaceful
Rational

FINDING MY HAPPY PLACE

Positive Characteristics

Positive Psychology has emerged in recent decades. It focuses on enhancing your well-being by shifting attention to what goes right in life. What is good about life is as authentic as what is bad and therefore merits attention.

Consider the suggestions below:

Adaptable	Excited	Loyal
Affectionate	Fair	Mature
Adventurous	Feisty	Mighty
Ambitious	Forgiving	Motivated
Appreciative	Friendly	Neat
Authentic	Fun	Nurturing
Balanced	Generous	Observant
Bold	Gentle	Open-Minded
Brave	Genuine	Optimistic
Calm	Gutsy	Organized
Capable	Happy	Original
Carefree	Helpful	Out-Going
Caring	Honest	Patient
Clever	Humble	Peaceful
Confident	Humorous	Persevering
Concerned	Imaginative	Persuasive
Considerate	Independent	Polished
Creative	Innovative	Practical
Curious	Insightful	Proactive
Dedicated	Intelligent	Protective
Dependable	Interesting	Proud
Determined	Intuitive	Prudent
Devoted	Joyful	Rational
Direct	Keen	Spunky
Disciplined	Kind	Tolerant
Easy-Going	Laid-Back	Thrifty
Empathetic	Leader	Unselfish
Energetic	Likable	Wise
Ethical	Logical	Witty
Exceptional	Loving	

Made in the USA
Coppell, TX
10 November 2021